Beatles For Recorder

CEA

Amsco Publications
London/New York/Sydney

Exclusive Distributors:
Music Sales Limited
8/9 Frith Street, London W1V 5TZ, England
Music Sales Corporation
225 Park Avenue South, New York, NY 10003, USA
Music Sales Pty. Limited
120 Rothschild Avenue, Rosebery, NSW 2018, Australia

This book © Copyright 1984 by
Amsco Publications
ISBN 0.7119.0542.8
Order No. NO 18434

Designed by Howard Brown
Cover photography by Peter Wood
Arranged and compiled by Robin De Smet

Music Sales complete catalogue lists thousands of titles and is free from your local music book shop, or direct from Music Sales Limited.
Please send a cheque or postal order for £1.50 for postage to Music Sales Limited, 8/9 Frith Street, London W1V 5TZ.

Printed in England by
Halstan & Co. Limited, Amersham, Bucks.

And I Love Her

Words & Music: John Lennon & Paul McCartney

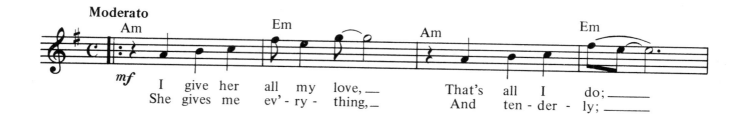

I give her all my love, ___ That's all I do; _____
She gives me ev'ry-thing, ___ And ten-der-ly; _____

And if you saw my love, ___ You'd love her too, And I love her. ___
The kiss my lov-er brings, ___ She brings to me, And I love her. ___

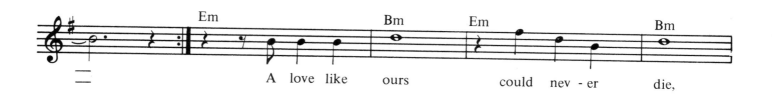

___ A love like ours could nev-er die,

As long as I have you near_ me. _____ Bright are the

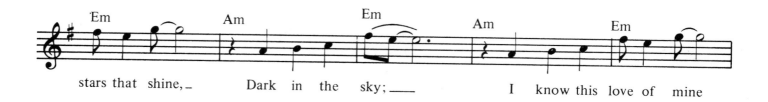

stars that shine, _ Dark in the sky; ___ I know this love of mine

Will nev-er die, And I love her. _____

All Together Now

Words & Music: John Lennon & Paul McCartney

Moderato

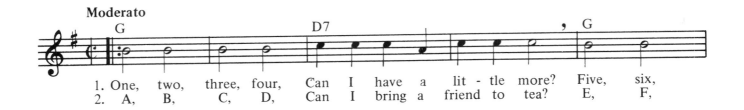

1. One, two, three, four, Can I have a lit-tle more? Five, six,
2. A, B, C, D, Can I bring a friend to tea? E, F,

sev-en, eight, nine, ten,___ I love you.___
G, H, I, J,___ I love you.___ Bom bom bom Bom-pa bom,

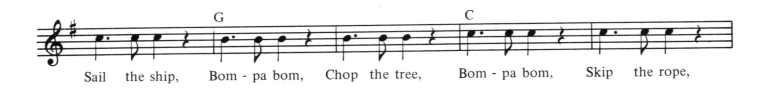

Sail the ship, Bom-pa bom, Chop the tree, Bom-pa bom, Skip the rope,

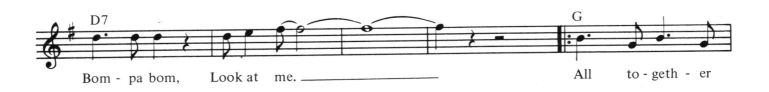

Bom-pa bom, Look at me.___ All to-geth-er

now, All to-geth-er now, All to-geth-er

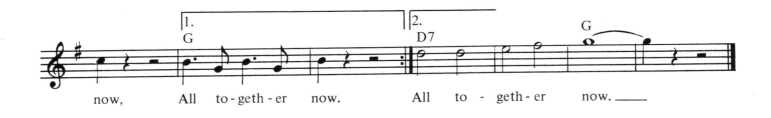

now, All to-geth-er now. All to-geth-er now.___

All My Loving

Words & Music: John Lennon & Paul McCartney

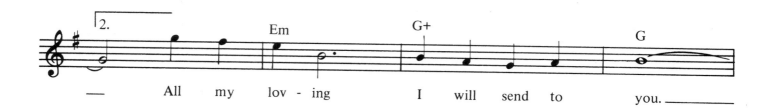

A Hard Day's Night

Words & Music: John Lennon & Paul McCartney

A Day In The Life

Words & Music: John Lennon & Paul McCartney

Moderately slow

I read the news to-day, oh boy, / A-bout a luck-y man who
He blew his mind out in a car, / He did-n't not-ice that the

made the grade. / And though the news was rath-er sad,
lights had changed. / A crowd of peo-ple stood and stared,

Well I just had to laugh. / I saw the pho-to-graph.
They'd seen his face be-fore.

No-bod-y was real-ly sure if he was from the House of Lords.

I saw a film to-day, oh boy, / The Eng-lish ar-my had just
I heard the news to-day, oh boy, / Four thou-sand holes in Black-burn

won the war. / A crowd of peo-ple turned a-way,
Lanc-a-shire. / And though the holes were ra-ther small,

But I just had to look. / Hav-ing read the
They had to count them all.

D.S. al Coda

book, I'd love to turn you on.

CODA

Now they know how man-y holes it

takes to fill the Al-bert Hall. I'd love to turn you on.

Hello Goodbye

Words & Music: John Lennon & Paul McCartney

Moderato

1. You say yes,_ I say no,_ You say stop,_ and I say go go
2. I say high,_ You say low_ You say why,_ and I say I don't

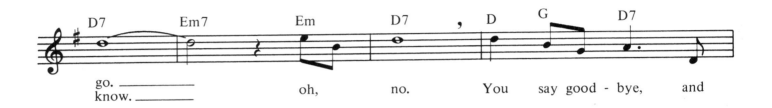

go. _____ oh, no. You say good-bye, and
know. _____ oh, no. You say good-bye, and

I say hel - lo. _____ hel - lo, hel - lo. _____ I don't know

why you say good-bye, I say hel - lo, _____ hel - lo, hel - lo, _____ I don't know

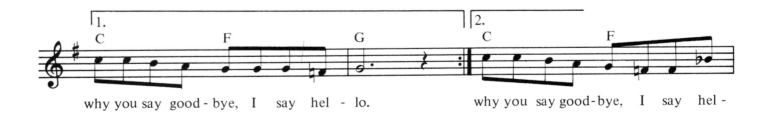

why you say good-bye, I say hel - lo. why you say good-bye, I say hel -

lo. _____ Hel-lo, hel - lo, _____ I don't know why you say good-bye, I say hel lo.

Hello Little Girl

Words & Music: John Lennon & Paul McCartney

When I see you ev'-ry day I say __ mm mm __ Hel-lo __ lit - tle girl. __
see you pas-sing by I cry __ mm mm __ Hel-lo __ lit - tle girl. __

__ When you're pas-sing on your way I say __ mm mm __ Hel-lo __ lit - tle girl.
__ When I try to catch your eye I cry __ mm mm __ Hel-lo __ lit - tle girl.

__ If I __ I send you flow - ers but you don't care, __

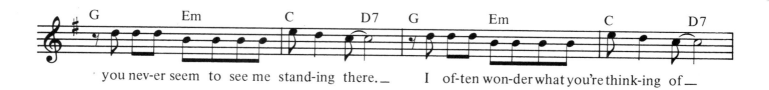

you nev-er seem to see me stand-ing there. __ I of-ten won-der what you're think-ing of __

I hope it's me, love, love, love. __ So I hope there'll come a day when you'll say __ mm mm __

you're my __ lit - tle girl, __ you're my __ lit - tle girl. __

Hold Me Tight

Words & Music: John Lennon & Paul McCartney

If I Fell

Words & Music: John Lennon & Paul McCartney

Moderato

If I give my heart to you, I must be sure from the ve - ry
trust in you, Oh, please don't run and hide if I love you

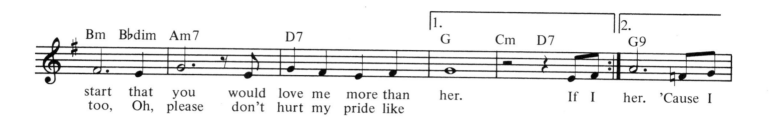

start that you would love me more than her. If I
too, Oh, please don't hurt my pride like her. 'Cause I

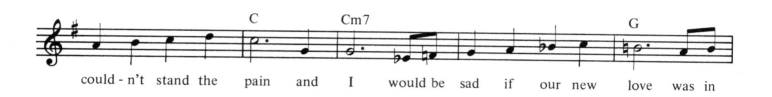

could - n't stand the pain and I would be sad if our new love was in

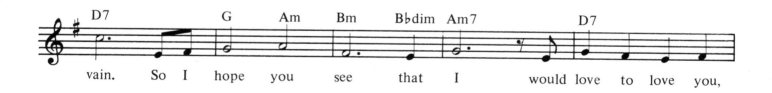

vain. So I hope you see that I would love to love you,

and that she will cry when she learns we are two. If I

rall.

fell in love with you (If I fell in love with you.)

I've Just Seen A Face

Words & Music: John Lennon & Paul McCartney

I Want To Hold Your Hand

Words & Music: John Lennon & Paul McCartney

Lady Madonna

Words & Music: John Lennon & Paul McCartney

Moderately

1.& 3. La - dy Ma - don - na, chil - dren at your feet,
2. La - dy Ma - don - na, ba - by at your breast,

Won - der how you man - age to make ____ ends meet? ____
Won - der how you man - age to feed ____ the rest. ____

Who finds the mon - ey when you pay the rent,
La - dy Ma - don - na, ly - ing on the bed,

Did you think that mon - ey was ____ hea - ven sent? ____
Lis - ten to the mus - ic play - ing ____ in your head. ____

____ Fri - day night ar - rives with - out a suit - case,
____ Tues - day af - ter - noon is nev - er end - ing, ____

Sun - day morn - ing creep - ing like a
Wednes - day morn - ing pa - pers did - n't

nun. Mon - day's child has
come. Thurs - day night your

learned to tie his shoe - lace. ____
stock - ings need - ed mend - ing. ____

D.C. al Fine last time

See how they run. ____
See how they run. ____

The Long And Winding Road

Words & Music: John Lennon & Paul McCartney

Michelle

Words & Music: John Lennon & Paul McCartney

Norwegian Wood

Words & Music: John Lennon & Paul McCartney

Ob-La-Di, Ob-La-Da

Words & Music: John Lennon & Paul McCartney

Moderately bright

1. Des - mond had a bar - row in the mar - ket place, ___
2. Des - mond takes a trol - ley to the jewel - ler's store, ___
3. Hap - py ev - er af - ter in the mar - ket place, ___

Mol - ly is the sing - er in a band. ___ Des - mond says to
Buys a twen - ty car - at gold - en ring. ___ Takes it back to
Des - mond lets the chil - dren lend a hand. ___ Mol - ly stays at

Mol - ly, girl I like your face ___ and Mol - ly says this as she takes him by the
Mol - ly wait - ing at the door ___ and as he gives it to her she be - gins to
home and does her pret - ty face ___ and in the eve - ning she still sings it with the

hand.
sing.   Ob - la - di, ___ ob - la - da, ___ life goes on, ___ yeh, ___
band.

La la how the life goes on. ___ Ob - la - di, ___ ob - la - da, ___

___ life goes on, ___ yeh, ___ La la how the life goes on. ___

Fine

___ In a cou - ple of years they have built a home ___ sweet home

With a cou - ple of kids run - ning

D.C. al Fine

in the yard ___ of Des - mond and Mol - ly Jones. ___

Penny Lane

Words & Music: John Lennon & Paul McCartney

Moderately bright

3. Back in Penny Lane: there is a fireman with an hour glass.
And in his pocket is a portrait of the Queen.
He likes to keep his fire engine clean, it's a clean machine.
Penny Lane is in my ears and in my eyes.
Full of fish and finger pies in summer meanwhile —

4. Back in Penny Lane: the barber shaves another customer.
We see the banker sitting, waiting for a trend.
And then the fireman rushes in from the pouring rain, very strange.
Penny Lane is in my ears and in my eyes.
Wet beneath the blue suburban skies I sit and meanwhile back:
Penny Lane is in my ears and in my eyes
Wet behind the blue suburban skies — Penny Lane.

She Loves You

Words & Music: John Lennon & Paul McCartney

1. You think you've lost your love,___ Well I saw her yes - ter-day-yi·yay, It's
2. said you hurt her so,___ Well she al-most lost her mind,___ And
3. know it's up to you,___ I think it's on - ly fair,___ And

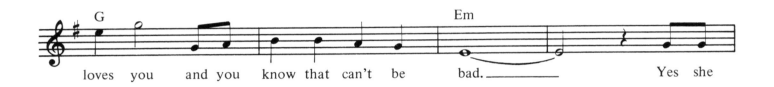

you she's think-ing of,___ And she told me what to say-yi-yay.
now she says she knows You're not the hurt - ing kind.___ She says she
Pride can hurt you too,___ A - po - lo - gize to her.___

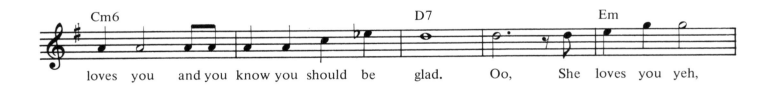

loves you and you know that can't be bad.___ Yes she

loves you and you know you should be glad. Oo, She loves you yeh,

yeh, yeh,_ She loves you yeh, yeh, yeh, And with a love like that you

know you should be glad._ She glad.___
You

She's Leaving Home

Words & Music: John Lennon & Paul McCartney

Waltz

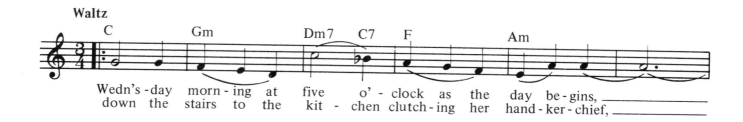

Wedn's-day morn-ing at five o'-clock as the day be-gins, _____
down the stairs to the kit-chen clutch-ing her hand-ker-chief, _____

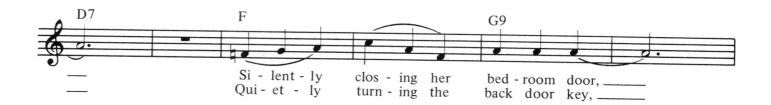

— Si-lent-ly clos-ing her bed-room door, _____
— Qui-et-ly turn-ing the back door key, _____

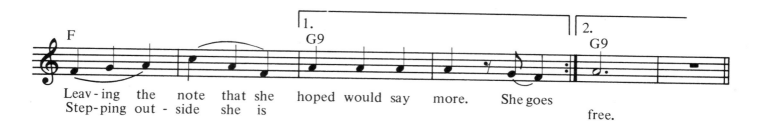

1. Leav-ing the note that she hoped would say more. She goes
Step-ping out-side she is

2. free.

CHORUS

She (We gave her most of our lives) is leav-ing (Sac-ri-ficed

most of our lives) _____ home. (We gave her ev'-ry-thing mon-ey could buy.)

She's leav-ing home af-ter liv-ing a-lone for so man-y years. _____

Strawberry Fields Forever

Words & Music: John Lennon & Paul McCartney

Thank You Girl

Words & Music: John Lennon & Paul McCartney

When I'm Sixty Four

Words & Music: John Lennon & Paul McCartney

Medium bounce

1. When I get old — er los - ing my hair —
2. I could be hand - y mend - ing a fuse —
3. Send me a post - card drop me a line —

man - y years from now. — Will you still be send - ing me a
when your lights have gone. — You can knit a sweat - er by the
stat - ing point of view. — In - di - cate pre - cise - ly what you

val - en - tine, — birth - day greet - ings, bot - tle of wine? —
fire - side, — Sun - day morn - ings, go for a ride. —
mean to say, — yours sin - cere - ly wast - ing a - way. —

If I'd been out — till quar - ter to three —
Do - ing the gar - den, dig - ging the weeds —
Give me an an - swer, fill in a form, —

would you lock — the door? — Will you still need — me,
who could ask — for more? —
mine for ev - er - more. —

will you still feed — me, when I'm six - ty four? —

Yellow Submarine

Words & Music: John Lennon & Paul McCartney

Yesterday

Words & Music: John Lennon & Paul McCartney

Can't Buy Me Love

Words & Music: John Lennon & Paul McCartney

2. I'll give you all I've got to give if you say you love me too.
   I may not have a lot to give but what I've got I'll give to you.
   For I don't care too much for money for money can't buy me love.

3. Say you don't need no diamond ring and I'll be satisfied.
   Tell me that you want those kind of things that money just can't buy.
   For I don't care too much for money for money can't buy me love.

From Me To You

Words & Music: John Lennon & Paul McCartney

Medium tempo

If there's an-y-thing that you ____ want, If there's
an-y-thing that you ____ want, If Like a

an-y-thing I can ____ do Just call on me ____ and I'll
heart that's oh, so ____ true. Just call on me ____ and I'll

send it a-long ____ With love ____ from me ____ to you. ____ If there's

I got arms that long to hold ____ you and keep you by my

side; I got lips that long to kiss ____ you and keep you sat-is-

fied. If there's an-y-thing that you ____ want, If there's an-y-thing I can ____ do, Just

call on me ____ and I'll send it a-long With love ____ from me ____ to you. ____

From A Window

Words & Music: John Lennon & Paul McCartney

Moderato

Late yes - ter - day night___ I saw a light___ shine from a win - dow,
I could-n't walk on ___ un - til you'd gone___ from your___ win - dow,

And as I looked a - gain your___ face came in - to sight.
I had to make you mine I ___ knew you were the one.

Oh I would be glad_____ just to love a love like that, _____

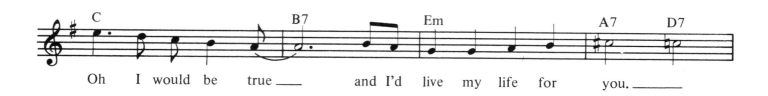

Oh I would be true ___ and I'd live my life for you. ___

So meet me to - night ___ just where the light___ shines from a win - dow,

And as I take your hand say that you'll _____ be mine to - night. _____

The Fool On The Hill

Words & Music: John Lennon & Paul McCartney

Slowly

Day af-ter day a - lone on a hill The man with the fool-ish grin is keep-ing
per-fect-ly still, But no-bod-y wants to know him they can see that he's just a fool And
he nev-er gives an an-swer. But the fool on the hill sees the sun go-ing down and the
eyes in his head see the world spin-ning round.

2. Well on the way head in a cloud
   The man of a thousand voices talking perfectly loud,
   But nobody ever hears him,
   Or the sound he appears to make
   And he never seems to notice.
   But the fool on the hill sees the sun going down
   And the eyes in his head see the world spinning round.

3. Day after day alone on a hill
   The man with the foolish grin is keeping perfectly still,
   And nobody seems to like him,
   They can tell what he wants to do
   And he never shows his feelings.
   But the fool on the hill sees the sun going down
   And the eyes in his head see the world spinning round.

4. Day after day alone on a hill
   The man with the foolish grin is keeping perfectly still
   He never listens to them,
   He knows that they're the fools
   They don't like him.
   But the fool on the hill sees the sun going down
   And the eyes in his head see the world spinning round.

Eleanor Rigby

Words & Music: John Lennon & Paul McCartney

Moderately

Ah, ____ look at all ____ the lone - ly peo - ple.

Play 3 times

1. El - ea - nor Rig - by picks up the rice ____ in the church ____

____ where the wed - ding has been, ____ Lives in a dream. ____

Waits at the win - dow, wear - ing the face ____ that she keeps ____

____ in a jar ____ by the door, ____ Who is it for? ____

All the lone - ly peo - ple ____ where do ____ they all ____ come from? ____

All the lone - ly peo - ple, ____ where do ____ they all ____ be - long? ____

2. Father McKenzie, writing the words of a sermon that no one will hear.
No one comes near. Look at him working, darning his socks in the night
When there's nobody there. What does he care? All the lonely people,
Where do they all come from? All the lonely people, where do they all belong?

3. Eleanor Rigby died in the church and was buried along with her name. Nobody came.
Father McKenzie wiping the dirt from his hand as he walks from the grave no one was saved.
All the lonely people, Where do they all come from? All the lonely people, where do they all belong?

Blackbird

Words & Music: John Lennon & Paul McCartney

Slow folk ballad

Black-bird sing-ing in the dead of night, Take these brok-en wings and learn to

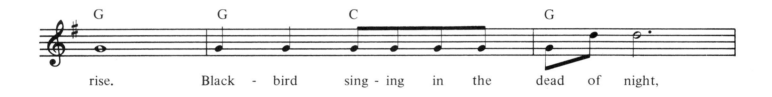

fly. All your life, _____ You were on-ly wait-ing for this mo-ment to a-

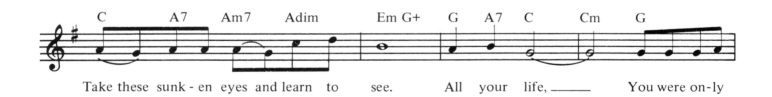

rise. Black-bird sing-ing in the dead of night,

Take these sunk-en eyes and learn to see. All your life, _____ You were on-ly

wait-ing for this mo-ment to be free. Black-bird fly. Black-bird

fly _____ in-to the light of a dark black _ night. _____

5/93 (15544)